WHEN WILL I STOP FAILING IN MANIFESTING MY DREAM LIFE?

RASI VERMA

Dedication

Firstly, I dedicate this book to myself. To remind me of the truth of life & manifestation again & again. So that, I do not forget it even during my difficult times! Because when we teach, we learn forever!

Secondly, I dedicate this book to the entire world. I want each one of you to know the truth of life & create your desired life every single second!

Immense love to each one of you!

Contents

What's On Our Holy Scriptures? xi

Acknowledgements xiii

Introduction xv

Preface xvii

Foreword xxi

Prologue xxv

1. ... 1

2. ... 2

3. ... 3

4. ... 4

5. ... 5

6. ... 6

7. ... 7

8. ... 8

9. ... 9

10. ... 10

11. ... 11

12. ... 12

13. ... 13

14. ... 14

15. ... 15

16. ... 16

17. ... 17

18. ... 18

Contents

19. ...	19
20. ...	20
21. ...	21
22. ...	22
23. ...	23
24. ...	24
25. ...	25
26. ...	26
27. ...	27
28. ...	28
29. ...	29
30. ...	30
31. ...	31
32. ...	32
33. ...	33
34. ...	34
35. ...	35
36. ...	36
37. ...	37
38. ...	38
39. ...	39
40. ...	40
41. ...	41
42. ...	42

Contents

43. ... 43
44. ... 44
45. ... 45
46. ... 46
47. ... 47
48. ... 48
49. ... 49
50. ... 50
51. ... 51
52. ... 52
53. ... 53
54. ... 54
55. ... 55
56. ... 56
57. ... 57
58. ... 58
59. ... 59
60. ... 60
61. ... 61
62. ... 62
63. ... 63
64. ... 64
65. ... 65
66. ... 66

Contents

67. ... 67

68. ... 68

69. ... 69

70. ... 70

71. ... 71

72. ... 72

73. ... 73

74. ... 74

75. ... 75

76. ... 76

77. ... 77

78. ... 78

79. ... 79

80. ... 80

81. ... 81

82. ... 82

83. ... 83

84. ... 84

85. ... 85

86. ... 86

87. ... 87

88. ... 88

89. ... 89

90. ... 90

Contents

The Answer!   91

What's On Our Holy Scriptures?

"And all things, whatsoever you shall ask in prayer,
believing, you shall receive."
- Matthew 21:22
"If you give thanks, I will give you more."
- Quran 14:7
"Whatever destinations and objects of pleasures, the
man, whose mind is free from impurities (negativity), he
obtains those destinations and those objects of pleasures."
- Mundakopanishad 3:1:10

Acknowledgements

Whom All I Want To Thank In My Life?

Before everyone, I want to thank me. I want to thank me to stay extraordinarily strong all the time. I want to thank me to have extraordinary desires. I want to thank me to be highly confident, fearless, ambitious, kind, generous, patient, intelligent & consistent in my efforts. I want to thank me for having an extraordinary vision, mind & understanding of life.

Next, I want to thank my graphic editors Shivam Yadav & Piyush Joshi for designing this book's graphics exactly the way I wanted it to be. Thanks for keeping immense patience with me, Shivam & Piyush. The best people to work with!

Now, a bucket full of thanks & gratitude to all of you who left me in my difficult times. Thanks to all the separations in my life, at home & outside. Thanks to all of you who mocked me, underestimated & disrespected me or my loved ones. You all are the reason behind my vigorous strength, development, growth & success, majorly! You all give me the reason to stand strong, never quit, stay consistent & surprise you all frequently. So, a real big thanks to you, my haters!

Now, the real person who taught me what strength is, what ambition is, what dreaming beyond normality is, what being focused & consistent is, & what the other components of success are, is my mother Rakhi Verma. I have not seen a more ambitious woman in my life till now, to be frank. She is a miracle in herself. I will have to write a separate essay on her. So, let's leap this for now. So, I want to thank her to be my mother, My Mother! It's in me through her, so I'm very thankful to my mother to be extraordinary.

I'm so so blessed to have hell supportive parents, amazingly supportive! At all cost! Trust me, we can't have a more supportive father! I have seen problems in my friends families, cousins and many a people's families related to parental support, not necessarily financial, but emotional & mental support. So, on a very serious note, I'm so so grateful to have over the top & extraordinarily supportive father Rajeev Verma!

Now, I want to thank my younger uncle Rajneesh Verma. He's an NITian, a monk & a genius! Yes, he quit his profession & became a monk to know his mind deeply! He's a moving encyclopedia! I'm so so thankul to him for existing. And I'm also thankful to my grandmother for giving birth to this man & making him a part of my family!

He's is the one whom I have my maximum conversation with, everyday. He's the closest one to me in my entire family. We enjoy each other's company discussing mind & life for hours. There's only learning & growing in my life. So, I'm surviving in a very healthy atmosphere overall. I'm thankful to all the people, my circle for my never-ending growth!

Last but not the least, I want to thank the Almighty, the Creator, the Universe for existing! I want to thank the Creator for blessing us all with the most powerful & the only tool that we need to create our life our way, that too, all for free - **That's Our Mind!**

Introduction

What's There In This Book?

Either you are new to manifestation or you have been trying to master it for long. If you are not new to it, I know you must have been trying to manifest a lot of things. Sometimes you manifest, sometimes you fail, or only a few desires get manifested and majority of them don't, or you tried doing it again and again but failed every single time!

Enough is enough! No more failing is allowed now. Let us all have fun together! You will stop failing in manifesting your deepest desire when you know The Answer! I promise you! I said it. It's done. Now it has to happen!

I don't want you to waste anymore of your time on this. You are here to know the secret.

In this book, you'll find the most precise meaning of manifestation and it's tool, the Law Of Attraction. You will get to know why you were failing in manifesting your desires till now. Lastly, now you will know the way to completely get rid of failing in manifesting your deepest desires! Permanently!

Preface

What Is Manifestation?

I know why you are here. Either you have failed many a times in manifesting your desires or you are the one who don't know what manifestation is. So, let me tell you what manifestation is!

Manifestation is the process of creating our desired life with the help of our vision and feelings. Not thoughts, precisely!

Why not thoughts, will reveal in the upcoming sequels. For now, let's focus on our vision and feelings!

Manifestation works on the principle of the Law Of Attraction.

The LOA is the most powerful law in this entire Universe. Just like gravity, it's always constantly moving around. It is working at this very second of our life. We are constantly in a state of development. We are creating our life in every second of each day. We are creating our future with every single thought, feeling and vision; either purposely or unconsciously. We can never pause from it. We can also not make a decision to not create as development never quits.

The LOA is the magnetic power that materializes through everybody and through everything in this Universe. Even the law of gravity belongs to the law of attraction. This law develops thoughts, ideas, individuals, situations, circumstances pand also the things we think of.

It is the power that creates the scenarios and circumstances we want. It is the power that brings in our life individuals that can help us with our plans.

If we are feeling happy, delighted, enthusiastic, satisfied or bountiful, then we are sending out positive energy. On the other hand, if we are feeling bored, nervous, stressed out, angry or depressed, we are sending out negative energy.

The LOA responds passionately to both these vibrations! It does not choose which one is better for us, it just reacts to whatever energy we produce. It gives us even more of the exact same! We get back exactly what we put out there.

Whatever we are assuming and feeling at a given point of time is actually our own demand to the Universe for more of the exactly same. Since, our vibrations will bring in energy back to us of the exact same frequency, we need to ensure that we are continuously sending energy, thoughts, vision and feelings that correspond with what we wish to be or experience!

Our vibrational frequency needs to be in tune with what we want to attract in life. If happiness, abundance as well as love are what we wish to attract then the vibrational frequencies of happiness, abundance and love are what we need to send out.

Now, I break the process of manifestation my way to some simple steps:

- Discover your deepest desires. Have the courage and confidence to have those desires. Ask or demand the Universe to fulfill them.
- Visualise yourself with these desires fulfilled in front of you.
- Feel deeply as if your desires just now got fulfilled right in front of you at this moment, where you are sitting or

standing right now.

- Know that the moment you saw and felt your desire, it got fulfilled right there. Only seeing and feeling was all that required to get it fulfilled.
- Show thankfulness and gratitude to the Universe, your Creator for fulfilling your desires this easily which was not possible for you alone!
- Now, forget about everything because your desires have already got fulfilled so what's more left there to think about?
- Now, this is the last and the most important step to manifestation. Plan the actions you should execute to get a step closer to your desires & start taking action right now, at this very moment. Just start it without a thought! This will keep you busy, detached from your desires and overthinking!

I will explain all these steps thoroughly and my way of following these steps in my upcoming sequels.

Foreword

Why Writing This Book?

Just laughing at my past and all of you out there who are sad at this very moment. Feeling pity on you of being sad when there is no requirement of it, in fact! Basically, you are not at fault. You guys just have lack of knowledge. Your concept on the mind and life is not clear. You guys just need to have complete and precise knowledge about the mind & life. That's all. And you all don't need to struggle anymore when I'm there for you all. I have done your part of the homework too!

I was an introvert since childhood. I didn't at all like to move out and socialise with people. My fight used to happen very quickly with classmates, cousins, and other children out there. I used to lose people quickly, at home as well as outside. I consider this as one of the biggest failures of my life!

Since childhood, I was a multi-tasker and immensely creative. I was very ambitious. I wanted everything in my life since the very beginning. My desires had & have no limit. Sky is the only limit for me. People used to call me impractical because I always had wild dreams.

Gradually, on getting more and more into manifestation, I started enjoying it seeing the positive results in the beginning. Now, everything has it's own pros and cons. Due to innumerable desires, I started practising manifestation vigorously. Consequently, I used to remain extremely desperate about the results. I remained attached to the results and overthinked all the time. It led to failure majority of the time. Now, failure led to extreme sadness when expectations were not met frequently!

I highly enjoy surprising people by breathtaking achievements who underestimate or disrespect me. I don't argue with people. I answer them with beautiful surprises.

LOL. The very first reason behind starting gaining knowledge about manifestation is a rejection! I couldn't be the school captain at the last moment from my batch where I tried giving my 100% in academics as well as curricular activities for last 5-6 years. I was an introvert as well as highly ambitious. My ego was hurt very very badly.

I was very sad because we get this chance only once during our entire school era. Although I failed ultimately, but the night before the selection, I was very nervous. I searched on Google 'how to make anything possible' & for me, the desire was to get selected as the school caption and that's where things started!

I am practising manifestation since childhood but have failed majority of the time. I always had this problem of overthinking. Extreme overthinking! I was never consistent in my process. I got bored very easily. I used to restart again and again.

I always wanted to give over the top results to my parents at the same time. Then came the worst part of my life! I lost my only sibling, my 21 years old twin brother Risi Verma last year while he was completing his L.L.B. degree in Chandigarh. I had not thought that my parents would survive. I thought everything was over. Our life was over. We wouldn't survive. Losing my handsome young brother was the worst nightmare of my life. I can never face anything worse than this!

But life didn't end there. I didn't let it. I stood up for my brother. His dreams were left to be fulfilled. I couldn't let my genius brother's haters rejoice of him being no more and his dreams remaining unfulfilled. I can never let my brother's dreams be dishonored. I decided to live for him and fulfill all his dreams. This biggest sorrow of my life became my biggest strength. My life changed here!

After losing my brother, I restarted again and I never knew that this was my last restart! I began with my failures this time. I started focusing on my mistakes in the process of manifestation. I started observing my own way of doing it, precisely. I used to compare & observe the differences in my process of doing it, the time when I failed & the time when I 100% manifested the results. I started making notes of all my observations.

After a long time since I started analysing my mistakes, I was really shocked to finally get the answer why I was failing in manifestation frequently. Was shocked to know the solution of not failing again in it. The answer was this simple!

One thing I got sure in, that day, was that the hardest questions have the simplest answers!

Now, when I know how to get rid of failure in manifestation, I can't at all see any girl or any woman or family or a boy or any man crying out there or in grief when there is no need to, at all cost, trust me!

I want to see each and everyone of you smiling, rejoicing, happy, satisfied, confident, having peaceful sleeps at night!

Thus, I can't wait to tell you exactly when you will stop failing in manifesting your dream life!

Prologue

The Book With 90 Blank Pages!

I don't want you to read huge essays on manifestation. You have already done a lot of that and still failed many a times which is why you are here reading this book. I don't even want anyone of you to waste anymore of your time reading innumerable books and pages and again going back to zero. I want to give you the solution with no more wait!

The old people are regretting and they wish they had more time. When we get old, we also have the chances to regret and wish we had more time. So, whatever time we have now, let's utilise every second of it. Time is running out slowly. If starting late, we can win, then if we start from now, then we can do a lot more extra!

When I'm there with you, you don't need to read lengthy books to get the simplest answer of life! I believe in simplication. So, let me simplify your life for you!

I have tried using the most easy and simple words for you all to understand everything precisely. Also, I have tried to make this a to-the-point communication with you. My intention is to make you jump to the solution to life & manifestation immediately rather than wasting your precious time in over-long readings.

You may call this 'The book with 90 blank pages!'
Now, let's jump to page 91 and reveal the only and biggest secret to life and manifestation:
'When Will I Stop Failing In Manifesting My Dream Life?'...

CHAPTER ONE

...

CHAPTER TWO

...

...

CHAPTER THREE

...

...

CHAPTER FOUR

•••

•••

CHAPTER FIVE

...

...

CHAPTER SIX

...

...

CHAPTER SEVEN

...

...

CHAPTER EIGHT

...

...

CHAPTER NINE

...

CHAPTER TEN

...

CHAPTER ELEVEN

•••

CHAPTER TWELVE

...

CHAPTER THIRTEEN

...

...

CHAPTER FOURTEEN

...

...

CHAPTER FIFTEEN

...

...

CHAPTER SIXTEEN

...

...

CHAPTER SEVENTEEN

...

...

CHAPTER EIGHTEEN

...

...

CHAPTER NINETEEN

• • •

...

CHAPTER TWENTY

...

...

CHAPTER TWENTY-ONE

...

...

CHAPTER TWENTY-TWO

...

...

CHAPTER TWENTY-THREE

•••

...

CHAPTER TWENTY-FOUR

...

...

CHAPTER TWENTY-FIVE

...

...

CHAPTER TWENTY-SIX

...

CHAPTER TWENTY-SEVEN

...

...

CHAPTER TWENTY-EIGHT

...

...

CHAPTER TWENTY-NINE

...

CHAPTER THIRTY

...

...

CHAPTER THIRTY-ONE

...

...

CHAPTER THIRTY-TWO

•••

CHAPTER THIRTY-THREE

...

...

CHAPTER THIRTY-FOUR

...

...

CHAPTER THIRTY-FIVE

...

CHAPTER THIRTY-SIX

•••

...

CHAPTER THIRTY-SEVEN

...

...

CHAPTER THIRTY-EIGHT

•••

...

CHAPTER THIRTY-NINE

•••

...

CHAPTER FORTY

...

CHAPTER FORTY-ONE

...

CHAPTER FORTY-TWO

...

...

CHAPTER FORTY-THREE

...

...

CHAPTER FORTY-FOUR

...

...

CHAPTER FORTY-FIVE

•••

...

CHAPTER FORTY-SIX

...

...

CHAPTER FORTY-SEVEN

•••

...

CHAPTER FORTY-EIGHT

•••

...

CHAPTER FORTY-NINE

...

...

CHAPTER FIFTY

...

...

CHAPTER FIFTY-ONE

...

...

CHAPTER FIFTY-TWO

...

...

CHAPTER FIFTY-THREE

...

...

CHAPTER FIFTY-FOUR

•••

CHAPTER FIFTY-FIVE

...

...

CHAPTER FIFTY-SIX

...

...

CHAPTER FIFTY-SEVEN

•••

...

CHAPTER FIFTY-EIGHT

...

...

CHAPTER FIFTY-NINE

...

...

CHAPTER SIXTY

...

...

CHAPTER SIXTY-ONE

•••

...

•••

CHAPTER SIXTY-THREE

...

...

CHAPTER SIXTY-FOUR

•••

...

CHAPTER SIXTY-FIVE

...

...

CHAPTER SIXTY-SIX

...

...

CHAPTER SIXTY-SEVEN

...

...

CHAPTER SIXTY-EIGHT

...

...

CHAPTER SIXTY-NINE

...

...

CHAPTER SEVENTY

...

...

CHAPTER SEVENTY-ONE

...

...

CHAPTER SEVENTY-TWO

...

...

CHAPTER SEVENTY-THREE

...

...

CHAPTER SEVENTY-FOUR

...

...

CHAPTER SEVENTY-FIVE

...

...

CHAPTER SEVENTY-SIX

...

...

CHAPTER SEVENTY-SEVEN

...

...

CHAPTER SEVENTY-EIGHT

...

...

CHAPTER SEVENTY-NINE

...

CHAPTER EIGHTY

...

...

CHAPTER EIGHTY-ONE

...

...

CHAPTER EIGHTY-TWO

...

...

CHAPTER EIGHTY-THREE

...

...

CHAPTER EIGHTY-FOUR

...

...

CHAPTER EIGHTY-FIVE

...

...

CHAPTER EIGHTY-SIX

...

...

CHAPTER EIGHTY-SEVEN

...

...

CHAPTER EIGHTY-EIGHT

CHAPTER EIGHTY-NINE

•••

...

CHAPTER NINETY

...

...

The Answer!

See, now that you know what manifestation is, you either believe in it or you don't. And even if you believe in it, there can be recurring doubts about it, which leads to overthinking, attachment, desperation, fear & ultimately failure in manifesting the results and which is why you are here!

You are failing in manifesting your deepest desires because either you don't believe in it or you have frequent doubts about it.

So, here again the question arises -

Why to believe in manifestation & it's tool, the Law Of Attraction?

So, I would like to start answering the biggest question of all time with a few questions. Just answer me these simple questions:

What does it take you to believe that everything happens in this Universe as a result of the Law Of Attraction? Do you think everything is happening randomly in this Universe?

What does it take you to have the courage to discover & reveal your own deepest desires? Is it illegal? Are you being asked someone else's desires or your own?

What does it take you to write down & make a note of your own goals right now? Are we talking about someone else's goals or your own?

What does it take you to ask or demand from your Universe, your Creator, your own Heavenly Parent limitlessly? Is the Universe charging you huge bucks for this?

What does it take you to visualise or see your own self in a situation as if the Universe has already given you everything in your hands that you have ever asked for? Are you looking ugly with your dreams in your hands?
What does it take you to exactly feel the way as if Universe has already given you whatever you ever wanted? Are you feeling sad in your Lamborghini?
What does it take you to believe that everything is already yours whatever you asked the Universe for? Is it costing you anything?
What does it take you to thank your Universe, your Parent Creator for giving you everything that you ever asked for? Will you fight with your Creator for creating a Dreamy Villa for you or you will thank him for it?
What does it take you to let go & leave everything in the hands of your Universe, the Creator? When the Creator has already freed you from all the burden, mentioning in the Holy Scriptures, then why you purposely trying to take tension on yourself?
What does it take you to detach your ownself from everything at this moment? Are you enjoying overthinking & the headache when you already have the option to purposely think about something else & become happy instantly?
What does it take you to forget about everything & get busy taking actions in favour of your own goals right now? Will you get more distant from your desires that way?
What does it take you to repeat your ask-believe-receive process for 10mins every day after your lunch? Is it bad for your mental health?
What does it take you to repeat your manifestation meditation for 5mins every night before sleeping? Will it spoil your sleep?

What does it take you to read 5 positive affirmations every morning while leaving for work? Will it ruin your day?

What does it take you to listen to your favourite energetic song every morning while you are brushing your teeth? Will it make you sad?

What does it take you to forgive yourself & everyone else & let it all go right now? Will it make you unhappy?

What does it take you to be kind to yourself and everyone else from now onwards? Will people hate you for this?

What does it take you to be positive all the time starting from this very moment? Will it make you look sad in front of others?

What does it take you to be happy all the time from this very moment? Will it make you mentally unhealthy?

What does it take you to feel energetic all the time from now onwards? Will it make you look ugly in front of others?

What does it take you to forget about others & focus on your life starting right now? Were you born together or will you die together with that person whom you are talking about right now?

What does it take you to pay attention to this very minute rather than today, tomorrow or yesterday? Will it destroy your present?

What does it take you to forget about yesterday knowing that it's never coming back & bothering you? Will focusing on yesterday be more profitable than focusing on now?

What does it take you to believe that the only time that exists is present & there's no past or future, only the memories exist because of our experience? Are you able to see the past & future? Are you not able to see the present & now moment? You decide.

What does it take you to believe that there is no such thing like karma? People are living happily everafter. How can someone else's Karma affect anyone else? Karma doesn't exist because past doesn't exist. Memories do! Memories let us think of the impression created by the concerned people in those memories. Mind is the creator of everything, not Karma!

What does it take you to be highly confident? Are you getting charged for it?

What does it take you to have faith? Will having faith make you unhappy?

What does it take you to be disciplined? Will it ruin your daily life?

What does it take you to repeat your daily routine consitently? Will it take you far away from your goals?

What does it take you to be patient? Will it have a negative impact on your mental health?

So, what does it take you to do all this? How many bucks are you being charged for to do all this? In how many ways all the above affect you negatively? What does it take you to believe that the Law Of Attraction is responsible for the creation of every moment of your life? How much you are being charged for believing in the truth of life & what all negative impacts does it have on you?

Nothing! Absolutely nothing!

You are not getting charged anyway! In this world where everyone is struggling to bargain for the things they want to buy, how come you don't want to buy your own dream life for free? It's not for him or her or anyone else. It's for you! Love, Money, Abundance, Happiness everything is available for free! Then how come you are not willing to buy them all? Even the richest person will grab anything precious that's available for free! Then why not you? This is what you ever wanted right?

Buy it because it's available for free & it does not have any negative impact on your life at all cost!

Now, either you know & understand what manifestation is or you don't believe in it or doubt it even after knowing & understanding it.

Now, for instance, you don't believe in manifestation & it's tool, the Law Of Attraction at all or you doubt it even if you understand it. So, tell me what worse will happen if you are happy, positive, attractive, energetic, courageous, busy, detached from desperation, trust & thank your Creator, work towards your goals, forgive yourselves & others, patient, repeat your daily routine consistently, disciplined, believe only in present moment & that no time exists other than present moment & focus only on your life? What will happen if you focus only on what you want actually? Will you die? -

No! You'll remain distracted from negativity & impossiblity. You'll get closer & closer to your goals. You'll be relaxed, peaceful & happy. Once you happy, you'll keep everyone happy!

Now, what good will happen if you are sad, negative, chase everything, depressed, coward, idle, desperate as hell, don't believe in our Creator, have no goals, spread hatred, impatient, have a messed uplife with no organised routine, indisciplined, don't even understand what present moment is & always keep on thinking about past & future which is not even visible, have least interest in our own life & enjoy focusing on other's life more? What's the consequence of focusing on negativity or things you dont't want? -

You'll clearly be stressed, afraid, insecure, irritated, will misbehave with your parents, spouse, friends, colleagues & everyone. Will you be even able to survive this way?

So, let's take a chance. You decide. What will you choose?

Your life is just a matter of your choices & decisions only.

Which one is the better option? Positive or Negative? Either you understand manifestation & LOA precisely & meditate on it or even if you don't believe in it then also the entire manifestation process will clearly lead you to happiness only. But if you don't believe in it & avoid this truth of life, then you definitely be closer to grief & destruction. Because LOA is constantly working all the time in your life like the law of gravity, whether you believe in it or not.

Hence, believing in manifestation is the better option. Now, if you choose manifestation & it promises you to provide anything & everything with no terms & conditions & that too for free then why don't you try the manifestation steps for free?

Because any which way the entire process will make you happier & more attractive even if it was not true, for instance!

Now, once you know what manifestation & it's tool, the Law Of Attraction is, and why doubting it is not a better option, you will now dedicatedly choose manifestation & certainly not fail in believing in it & hence you will manifest all your deepest desires from now onwards! I promise!

In the upcoming sequels, I will explain my own simplified process of manifestation using the LOA, thoroughly. I will also explain what 'thought' is, it's origin & how to get rid of negative thoughts permanently which is the only interruption in the present moment.